BLM-AK-PT-86-024-8351-028

Beaver Creek
National Wild River
Cultural Resources Inventory

by Susan Will

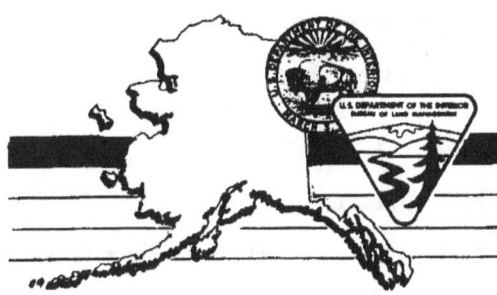

Open File Report 19

BUREAU OF LAND MANAGEMENT
A L A S K A

June 1986

OPEN FILE REPORTS

The category of "Open File Report" is used by BLM-Alaska to identify the results of inventories or other investigations that are made available to the public outside the formal BLM-Alaska technical publication series. These reports include preliminary or incomplete data that are not published or distributed in quantity but are available for public inspection at BLM offices in Alaska, the USDI Resources Library in Anchorage, and the various libraries of the University of Alaska.

THE AUTHOR

Susan M. Will is an archeologist working in the BLM's Yukon Resource Area, Fairbanks, Alaska.

ABSTRACT

Following a Class I literature search, which provided background information on the cultural resources of the entire river, Class II field inventory work for the portion of the Beaver Creek National Wild River managed by the Bureau of Land Management (BLM) was conducted. A single cultural site was found which consisted of a hearth/tent ring with no associated artifacts. In addition, information was obtained from a local resident about a mastodon or mammoth site along the river where bones had eroded out of a bluff. No paleontological material was available for examination and no cultural material had been reported in association.

INTRODUCTION

Beaver Creek is located in Interior Alaska, approximately 50 air miles north of Fairbanks (Fig. I). Its headwaters lie to the west of Mt. Prindle and from there it flows around the spine of the White Mountains and then through the Yukon Flats, emptying into the Yukon River near the village of Beaver. The Alaska National Interest Lands Conservation Act of December 2, I980 (ANILCA, P.L. 96-487) established the upper portion of Beaver Creek as a component of the National Wild and Scenic Rivers System (BLM I983:I).

The initial III-mile segment of the Beaver Creek National Wild River flows through a portion of the one million-acre White Mountain National Recreation Area (WMNRA). The river corridor within the WMNRA is managed by the BLM (Ibid:2). The remaining I6 miles of the Beaver Creek National Wild River lies within the Yukon Flats National Refuge and is managed by the U.S. Fish and Wildlife Service.

The Antiquities Act of I906 (P.L. 59-209; 34 Stat. 225; I6 U.S.C. 432, 433), the Historic Sites Act of I935 (P.L. 74-292; 49 Stat. 666; I6 U.S.C. 46I et seq), the National Historic Preservation Act of October I5, I966 (NHPA) (P.L. 89-665; 80 Stat. 9I5; I6 U.S.C. 470), the National Environmental Policy Act of I969 (NEPA) (P.L. 9I-I90; 83 Stat. 352; 42 U.S.C. 432I), the Federal Land Policy and Management Act of I976 (FLPMA) (P.L. 94-579; 90 Stat. 2743; 43 U.S.C. I70I), and the Archeological Resources Protection Act of I979 (ARPA) (P.L. 96-95) provide for the protection of cultural resources on public land. Executive Order II593 directs federal agencies to inventory their cultural resources and submit nominations to the National Register of Historic Places. Until this occurs, cultural resources are to be carefully considered. FLPMA also requires inventory of BLM lands for comprehensive resource planning. However, only Section I06 of NHPA directs agencies to take into account the affects of their actions on properties included in or eligible for the National Register and allow for comment by the Advisory Council on Historic Preservation. Procedures for complying with Section I06 and E.O. II593 are provided under 36 CFR 800.

BLM Manual 8I00 (I978) provides basic guidelines for cultural resources management within the agency. 8I00.02 B states that one of the program objectives is to insure that cultural resources are given full consideration in all land-use planning and management decisions. The first step in the BLM Manual process was the preparation of a Class I Inventory. This inventory, a cultural resources overview based on the existing information and known sites for the area, was completed in May of I984 (Will I984). Included in this inventory were the results of a survey of historic cabins along Beaver Creek which had

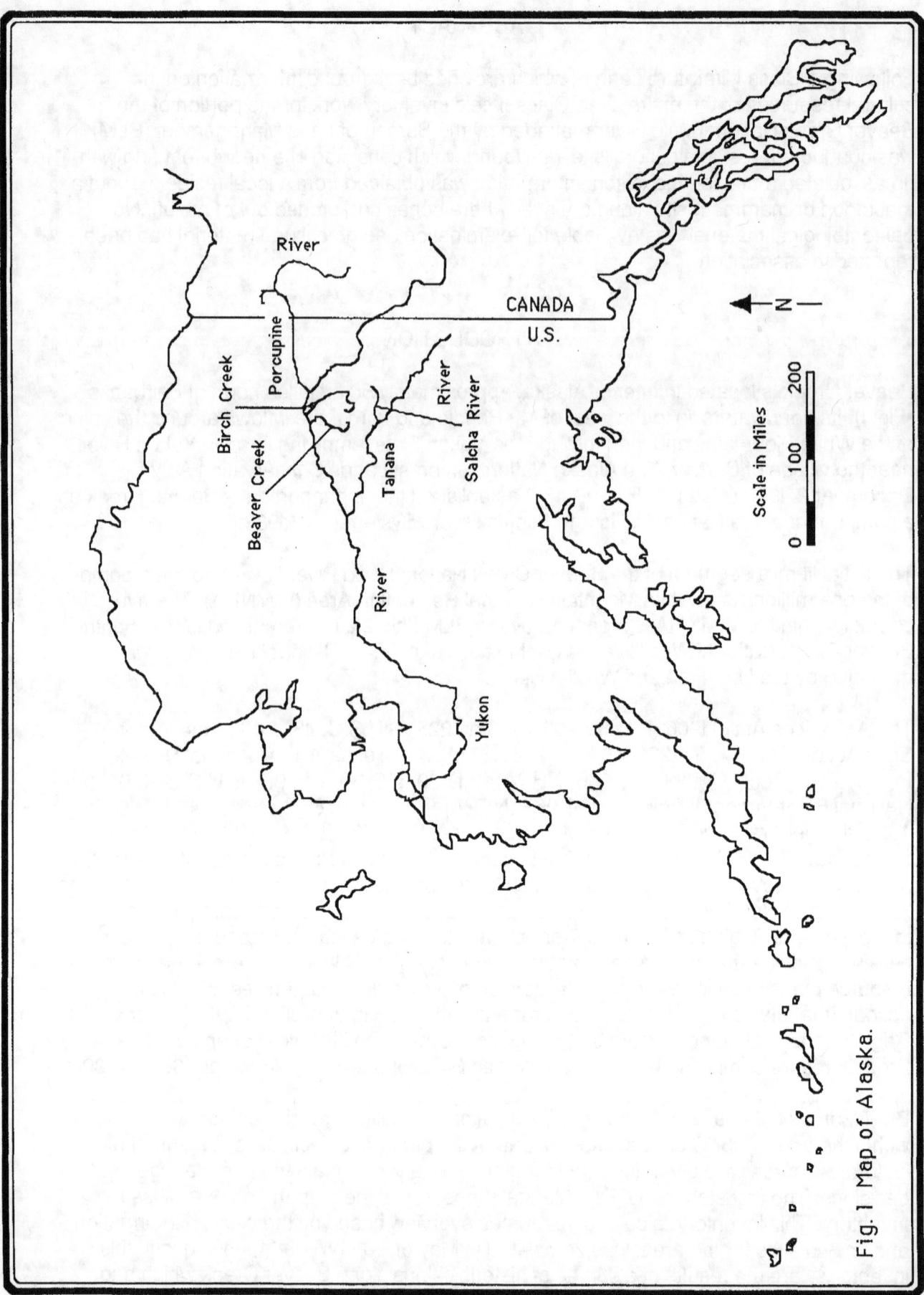

River

CANADA
U.S.

Birch Creek

Porcupine

River

Salcha River

Tanana

River

Yukon

N—

Scale in Miles

0   100   200

Fig. 1 Map of Alaska.

Beaver Creek

been conducted by BLM personnel during the summer of 1982. The second step required that a Class II or field sampling inventory be conducted. This inventory was completed in July of 1984 and the results of both inventories are combined in this report.

ENVIRONMENTAL BACKGROUND

A moderately swift, shallow stream surrounded by rolling hills in its upper reaches, Beaver Creek flows past the jagged limestone peaks of the White Mountains before slowing to a sluggish meandering river as it passes through the marshy Yukon Flats to the Yukon River, a total distance of 303 miles. Major tributaries include Bear, Champion, Nome, Trail, Wickersham, Fossil, and Victoria Creeks (Fig. 2). The region is characterized by alternating upland plateaus and marshy lowlands.

The climate of the area is sub-polar continental, where severe winters with extended periods of 50° F. above to 60° F. below zero are common, summers are short and warm with temperatures sometimes reaching over 80° F. above zero, and precipitation ranges only 5 to 20 inches per year. Freeze-up of the rivers and marshes takes place in October, while spring thaws occur during April through May.

Soils are generally shallow and stony, with discontinuous permafrost underlying much of the area. Vegetation, which is highly dependent upon soil conditions, ranges from treeless areas of alpine tundra in the higher elevations, to sparsely vegetated black spruce bogs, and open spruce- hardwood forest in drainages and upland plateaus.

Wildlife

Beaver Creek's fishery consists primarily of Arctic grayling. Northern pike, sheefish, and whitefish are also present in the lower reaches of the river. Wildlife in the area include moose, black and grizzly bear, Dall sheep, wolves, and caribou. Common furbearers include lynx, beaver, marten, wolverine, muskrat, and fox. Bird species present include willow ptarmigan, spruce grouse, Canada geese and other migratory waterfowl, golden and bald eagles, and the peregrine falcon, an endangered species.

Historical work on caribou in the area (Skoog 1956) indicates that the Steese and White Mountains areas were important calving, summering, and wintering areas. Murie (1935:6) estimated that the Steese-Fortymile herd may have numbered as many as a million animals during the early 1900's.

Historically, the Fortymile caribou herd has migrated in the spring from wintering areas in the Fortymile country to calving grounds south of Birch Creek and to the White Mountains east of Beaver Creek. Summer dispersal takes place shortly after calving and the animals move throughout the area. Fall migration finds these animals moving back to the southeast to the Fortymile country (Davis et al. 1978). Additional work by Durtsche (1983) indicates there is a small resident herd of caribou that winters in the upland country west of Beaver Creek and migrates to the White Mountains where calving occurs in the spring (Fig. 3).

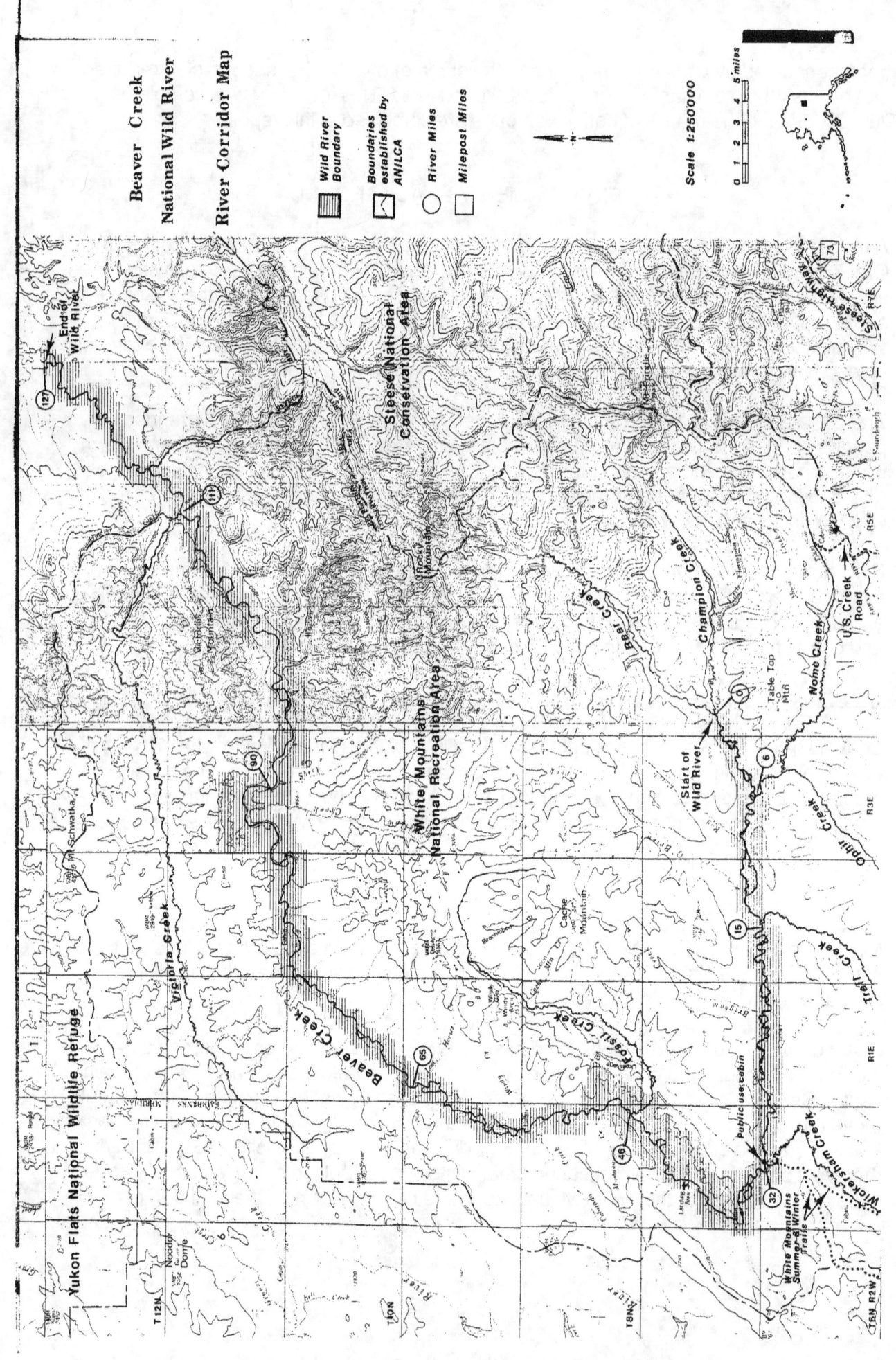

Beaver Creek
National Wild River
River Corridor Map

Wild River
Boundary

Boundaries
established by
ANILCA

○ River Miles

□ Milepost Miles

N

Scale 1:250000

0 1 2 3 4 5 miles

Yukon Flats National Wildlife Refuge

End of
Wild River

Steese National
Conservation Area

Rocky
Mountain

White Mountains
National Recreation Area

Victoria Creek

Beaver Creek

Bear Creek

Champion Creek

Nome Creek

U.S. Creek
Road

Table Top
Mtn

Start of
Wild River

Fossil Creek

Public use cabin

Cache
Mountain

Ophir Creek

Trail Creek

Wickersham Creek

White Mountains
Summer & Winter
Trails

Steese Highway

T12N

T10N

T8N

R2W

R1E

R3E

R5E

R7E

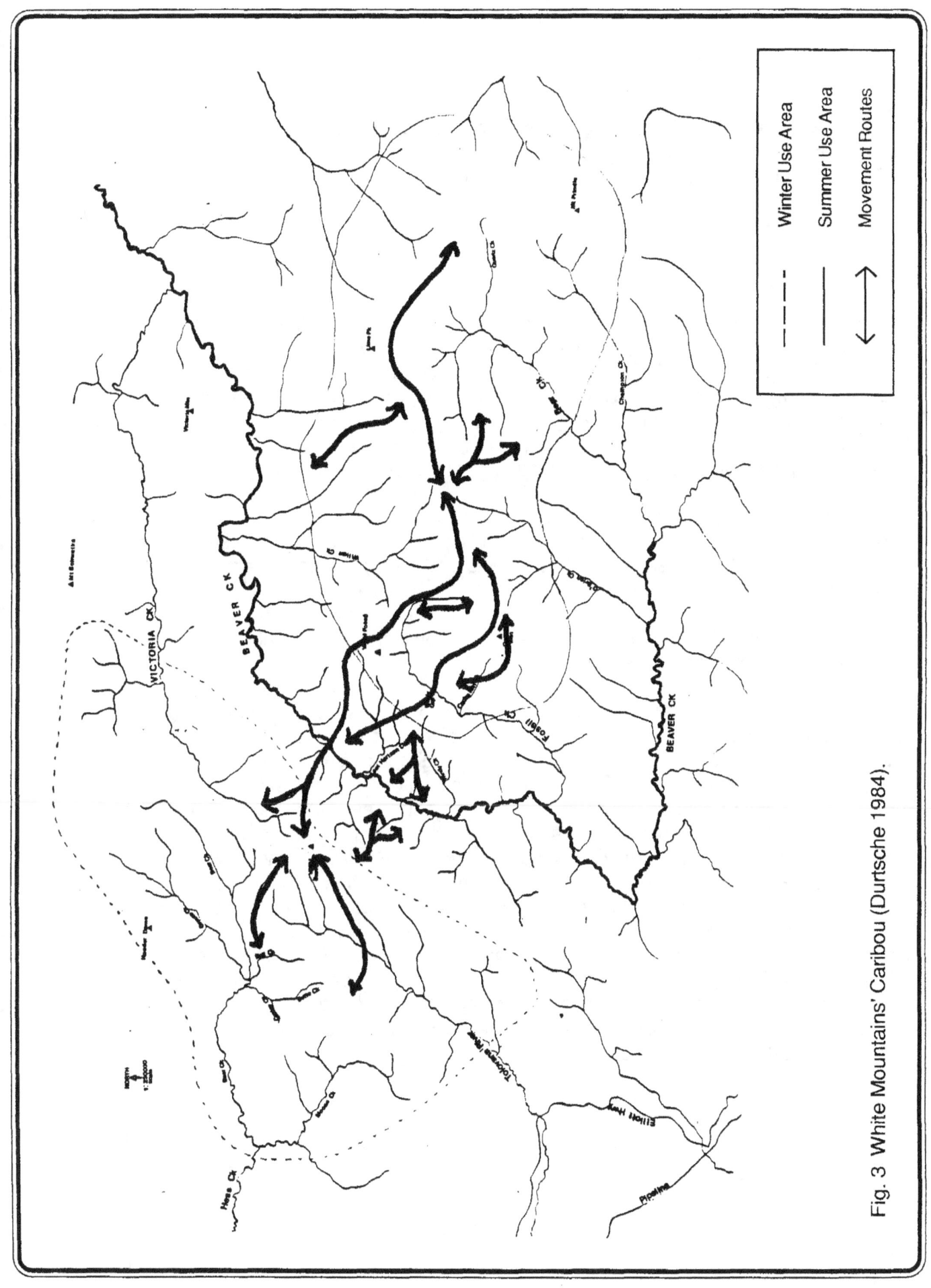

Fig. 3 White Mountains' Caribou (Durtsche 1984).

Geology

The Beaver Creek National Wild River flows out of the Tanana-Yukon Uplands and into the Yukon Flats. The Uplands is a structurally complex region of igneous, metamorphic, and sedimentary rocks ranging in age from Precambrian to Recent (Barker 1978:5).

From Nome Creek to the Big Bend area, the unconsolidated Quaternary deposits of the river valley overlie a metamorphic Pre-Silurian greenschist facies, Cambrian (?) quartzite, slate, and argillite.

Around the White Mountains, the river flows through a tectonically active fault zone. The first major fault occurs at the Big Bend where it crosses a band of Tolovana Limestone (the distinctive backbone of the White Mountains). Within this material are massive outcrops of chert which may well have served as raw material for early peoples, although chert outcrops are not evident along the river proper. The river then overlies a bank of Ordovician and Silurian volcanic rock before crossing the Beaver Creek Fault and entering a zone of Jurassic/ Cretaceous conglomerates, greywackes, and shales.

Downstream from this point Beaver Creek runs parallel to a series of active thrust faults and touches a zone of Lower Paleozoic mafic and ultramafic rocks (including serpentine) along the river's northern margin before continuing into the sedimentary bedrock of the Yukon Flats.

The structural activity in this area has resulted in erosion along the river which is evident in the unstable cutbanks and bluffs along its course.

Glacial geology work by Weber and Hamilton (1984) in the immediate Mt. Prindle area to the east of Beaver Creek (Fig. 2) indicates that there have been four separate Pleistocene glacial advances around the mountain. They are calling these the Prindle, Little Champion, American Creek, and Convert advances, in order from oldest to youngest (Ibid:42). Although this glacial activity is localized, the nature of the advances suggest that different regional and local climatic conditions have existed, which may be useful for future archeological interpretations. They are suggesting that the Prindle advances, which radiated to the southern and western valley systems from Mt. Prindle, may have been nourished by heavy snowfall from westerly and southerly winds. This may indicate that the Alaska Range was less of a barrier to maritime air masses during the early Pleistocene times than it is today. A long interval of active erosion took place after the Prindle glaciation. The three younger glaciations advanced to the northeast, largely following the existing drainage patterns in the immediate area and were less extensive than the early Prindle advance. This correlates to similiar glacial successions (Table I) described in central and northern Alaska (Ibid:47-48).

Mt. Prindle area	Alaska Range (Delta River Valley)	Alaska Range (Nenana River Valley)	Brooks Range	Approximate age (years B.P.)
Convert	Donnelly	Riley Creek	Walker Lake	
---		Middle Wisconsinan		(40,000)
American Creek	Delta	Healy	Itkillik	
---		Pelukian (125,000)		
Little Champion	---	'Lignite Creek'	Sagavanirktok River	
XXXXXXXXXXXXXXXXXXXXXXXXXXXXXXXXXXXXXXXXXXXXXXXXXXXXXXX				Kotzebuan (>175,000); (<250,000)
Prindle	Darling Creek	Browne erratics	Anaktuvuk River	
XXXXXXXXXXXXXXXXXXXXXXXXXXXXXXXXXXXXXXXXXXXXXXXXXXXXXXX				Anvilian (>700,000); (<1,800,000)
???	Tertiary tillites(?)	Pre-Browne erratics	Gunsight Mountain erratics	

------ Indicates minor erosion interval.
XXXXXXX Indicates major erosion interval.

Table I. Suggested correlation of Mt. Prindle glacial phases with other Alaskan glacial and sea-level records. (Hamilton and Weber 1984: Table 2.)

The Beaver Creek valley fill consists primarily of unconsolidated Quaternary alluvium with adjacent areas of loess, colluvium, and undifferentiated silts of Pleistocene and Holocene age (Chapmen, Weber, and Taber 1971: Open File Map #483).

The occurrence of the Pleistocene mammoth/mastodon bones near the mouth of Victoria Creek is undoubtedly associated with this valley fill and may have been redeposited.

PREHISTORY

As a summary, Cook's description of the prehistory for central Alaska still applies:

> In general terms, known sites in interior Alaska may be placed into three broad categories of cultural history: (I) historic or late prehistoric occupations, rather definitely Athabaskan in nature, (2) an older cultural stratum which may or may not, be early or ancestral Athabaskan, and (3) a vaguely defined early period. [Cook 1975:125]

Work by Hopkins (1967) and others has concluded that, during the late Wisconsin glaciation, Alaska and Siberia were part of a single continental land mass known as Beringia. Much of the ice-free interior of Alaska at that time consisted of a steppe-tundra environment (Ager 1975) which supported such animals as bison, horse, and mammoth (Guthrie 1968). Due to the presence of these large game animals, the land also supported people.

Work by West at Tangle Lakes and Donnelly Ridge (Fig. 4) has resulted in the definition of an important artifact assemblage known as the Denali complex. This complex has been identified as existing between 11,000 and 8,000 years ago (West 1981). It contains such characteristic elements as distinctive wedge-shaped microblade cores, burins made on flakes (Donnelly burins), biconvex bifacial knives, blades, and *tchi-thos* (West 1981). Sites bearing such materials are widespread in Alaska.

One of the earliest firmly dated interior Alaska sites, Dry Creek, dates to approximately 11,000 B.P. (Thorson and Hamilton 1977:166). Component I of this site, located along the northern flanks of the Alaska Range (Fig. 4), contains cultural material similar to that found in the lowest levels at Healy Lake (Fig. 4). This material, known as the Chindadn complex, differs from the Denali complex in that a different form of bifacial projectile or knife is present. Chindadn points date between 11,000 and 9,000 years ago (Cook 1975).

Work by Le Blanc at the Rat Indian Creek site along the Porcupine River in the Yukon Territory indicates that the site can be integrated into the existing prehistoric framework for the northern Yukon and other areas of the western subarctic (Le Blanc 1984:vii). He proposed two phases which accomodate the components at Rat Indian Creek as well as other middle Porcupine sites. The earlier, the Old Chief Phase, extends from ca. 900 B.C. to A.D. 700; the later, the Klo-kut Phase, begins about A.D. 700 and continues through the arrival of European traders. The latter includes the level 5 component at Rat Indian Creek and the prehistoric levels from the Klo-kut site. The Klo-kut site (Fig. 4), a stratified Athabaskan site in the Yukon Territory was occupied throughout the last 1,000 to 1,500 years (Morlan 1973).

Le Blanc's conclusion about these site comparisons describe a relationship which has been referred to as the "Athabaskan Tradition":

> External comparisons indicate that the Klo-cut Phase is closely related to such well-known sites as upper component Dixthada, Kavik, and several other sites throughout the northwest. Collectively, these late prehistoric manifestations can be considered as a broadly defined technocomplex spanning the period from roughly A.D. 700 to the mid ninteenth century. Although less well represented, the earlier Old Chief Phase exhibits relationships to a more restricted range of sites in Alaska (Itkillik complex at Onion Portage; the early componont at Minchumina) and southwest Yukon (Taye Lake phase components). [Le Blanc 1984:vii]

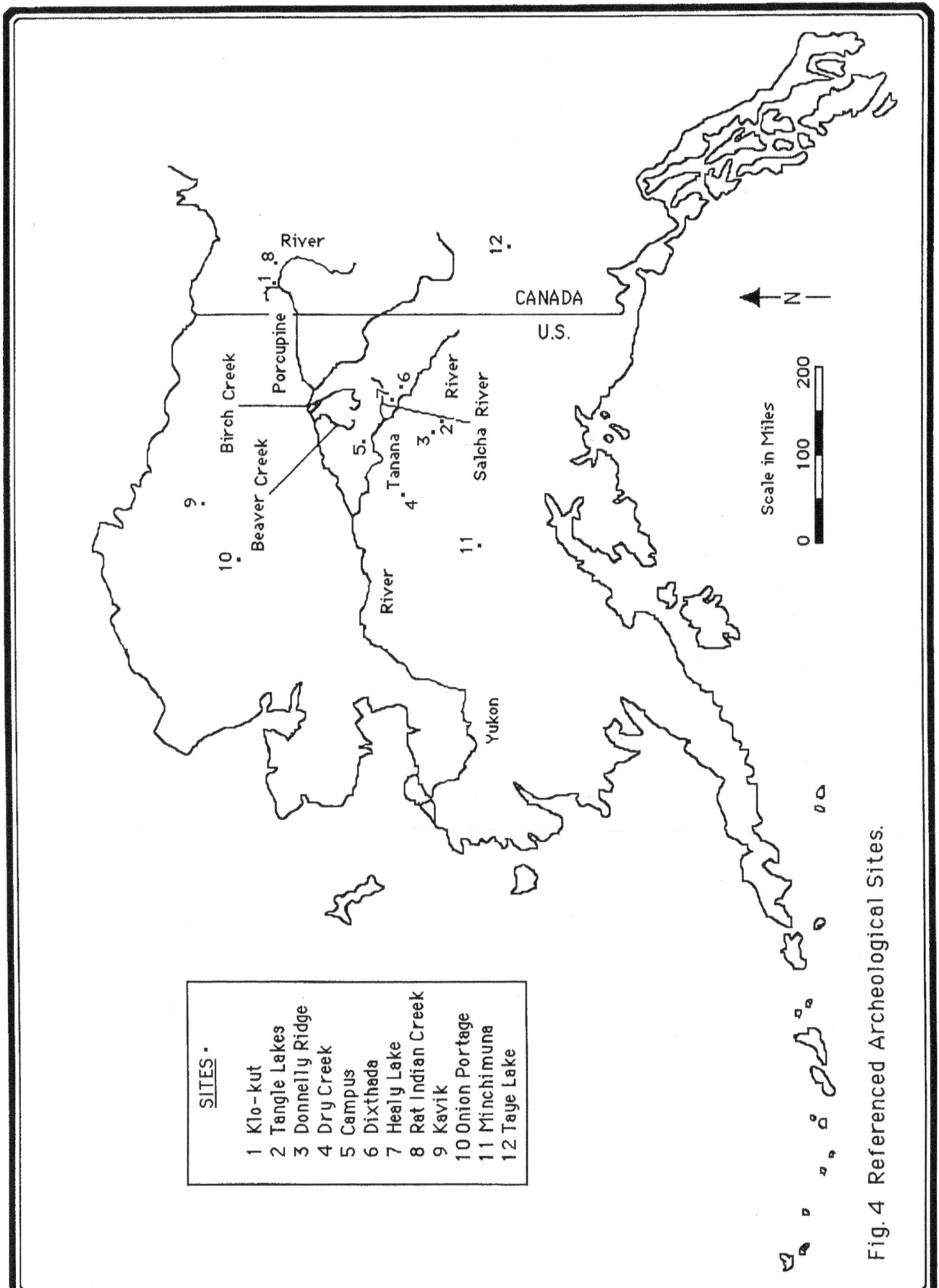

SITES ·

1 Klo-kut
2 Tangle Lakes
3 Donnelly Ridge
4 Dry Creek
5 Campus
6 Dixthada
7 Healy Lake
8 Rat Indian Creek
9 Kavik
10 Onion Portage
11 Minchimuna
12 Taye Lake

Fig. 4 Referenced Archeological Sites.

11

Ethnographic literature for the Beaver Creek area is extremely limited; nearby Birch Creek has received more attention. According to Orth (1971:118), the upper mouth of Birch Creek bore the Indian name "*Nocotocargut*", as reported by the Western Union Telegraph expedition. This river was also called the "She Beaver" (Baker 1901). Frederick Whymper, also a member of the expedition, visited Fort Yukon in 1868 and noted that "some of the *Gens de bouleau*, or Birch River Indians,...were present...." (Whymper 1966:223).

Osgood's monograph (1970), based on fieldwork undertaken during the summer of 1932, refers to the "Birch Creek" or "*Tennuth*" Kutchin in only two paragraphs but does provide a territorial map (Fig. 5). The monograph contains the following information:

> No complete study of the Kutchin nation can ever be made. Within twenty-five years of their first discovery, the Birch Creek Kutchin were annihilated by an epidemic of scarlet fever [Ibid:14-15].

> Both Birch Creek and Black River are roughly parallel to the Yukon but are mountain tributaries. The culture of these areas is that of people who live along small streams, turning periodically to the comfortable protection of their small isolated valleys [Ibid:16].

Most of Osgood's data came from informants at Circle and Fort Yukon (Ibid:4). The correlation between the Black River and Birch Creek is also mentioned in information provided by Birch Creek Jimmy, a resident of the small village at the mouth of Birch Creek (Schneider 1974 and 1976). The comparisons can also be extended to Beaver Creek, which has a similar environmental setting, flowing from the uplands into the Yukon Flats and emptying into the Yukon just below the mouth of Birch Creek.

Birch Creek Jimmy was born in 1884 at Chalkytsik and spent his early years on the Black and Porcupine Rivers. He remembered life as being extremely hard there; his family lived in a skin tent which they shared with another family. They had few trade goods, only muzzle loaders, and used bows and snares to hunt rabbits. People lived off moose, caribou, fish, and ducks - "which couldn't fly in the summer." (Schneider 1974)

By 1900, Jimmy was living at Birch Creek with his family and brother-in-law, who was the grandson of the famous Kutchin chief, Sahnyaati. They built their camp at the mouth of the Creek where two Hudson's Bay men, Anderson and Less, had formerly lived and operated a fish camp.

Whether or not these are the "Birch Creek Kutchin" to whom Osgood refers is unknown. According to Birch Creek Jimmy's description, their seasonal cycle was based in the lower reaches of Birch and Beaver Creeks where the country was quite different from the Black and Porcupine River country - "...kind of easy - a little bit fish, ducks, fur" (Schneider 1974). Once they had moved from the Black and Porcupine country to the mouth of Birch it appears that they didn't move far from the Flats; relying on that country to provide them

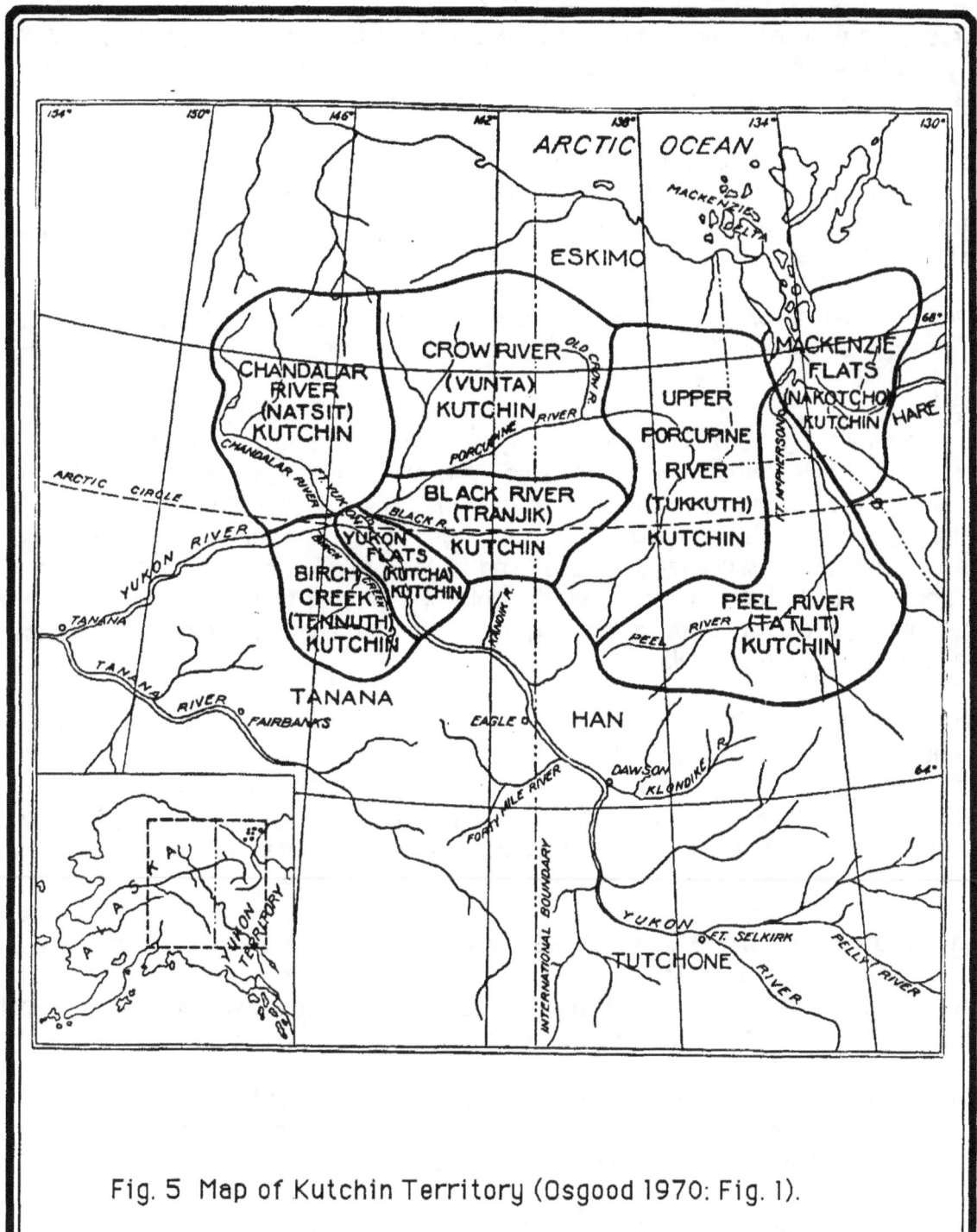

Fig. 5 Map of Kutchin Territory (Osgood 1970: Fig. 1).

with game and furs which they traded at Fort Yukon (Fig. 6). Fish were obtained in the creeks by using nets and traps.

However, Jimmy says that Sahnyaati' and his family moved around the country, living at Birch Creek, Fort Yukon, and Circle - "Circle country like their country" (Ibid. 1976:210). Raymond had encountered them in Rampart Canyon at a fish camp in 1869 which, as Schneider points out, was a good 160 miles down the Yukon.

It appears that boundaries and groups were hardly formal, at least by that time, and were based primarlily on the availability of resources. Sahnyaati' died in 1894 and had 10 wives "...one from Arctic Village, and one from Old Crow" (Ibid. 1974) According to Jimmy, they didn't all live together although Sahnyaati' did have a village at Circle.

Birch Creek residents consider themselves *Dendu Gwich'in*, who traditionally occupied the Yukon Flats region south of the Yukon and portions of the Crazy and White Mountains (Caulfield 1983:112).

According to David James, Birch Creek Jimmy's son, his father recounted that the original *Dendu Gwich'in* were "mountain people" who lived principally in the foothills of the White Mountains and utilized primarily caribou and sheep. The *Gwit'ee Gwich'in* were said to be the band who lived along Birch Creek and their name meant "people living under", perhaps referring to the fact that the band lived at the base of the White Mountains. The name *Dendu Gwitch'in* translates to mean "people of the other side" which is apparently a name assigned to the band by another group - not traditionally used by the band to describe itself (Caulfield 1983:112-113).

Prehistoric and late prehistoric use of the country by Native peoples is ultimately dependent on available resources. Prior to the coming of whites and the fur trade (with its emphasis on trapping and the need for fish to support dogteams), the major resource used in the upper Birch and Beaver Creek country was probably caribou. Following this would be moose, with lesser importance being placed on muskrat, beaver, fish, and waterfowl. McKennan (1969:34) supports this general theory.

Traditional use of the White Mountains area is reflected by the Kutchin place name *Luw ddhaa*, "white mountain", the *Dinkjuk vadzaih tthal* or moose and caribou fence located on the north side of the mountain, (Caulfield et al. 1983: map 2) and accounts of sheep hunting in the Victoria Mountain area before Birch Creek Jimmy's time (Caulfield 1983:112-113).

Murray (1910), McKennan (1969), Osgood (1970), and Nelson (1973) have all described the varying importance of caribou, aside from food, among different Kutchin people, depending on availability, for clothing and shelter, particularly in the past.

The few dogs kept by the Kutchin prior to the coming of the whites were used primarily for hunting and packing rather than pulling sleds (Nelson 1973:173 and Osgood 1970:59). Osgood states that, "Toboggans are not aboriginal. Men cut the trail ahead and women pull the sled, sometimes with the aid of boys. Only a few dogs are available because of the difficulty of feeding them and these are trained primarily for hunting" (Ibid.). Dogs were used to run down and hold caribou or moose at bay until the hunters could reach them, particularly in deep snow (Nelson 1973:173).

14

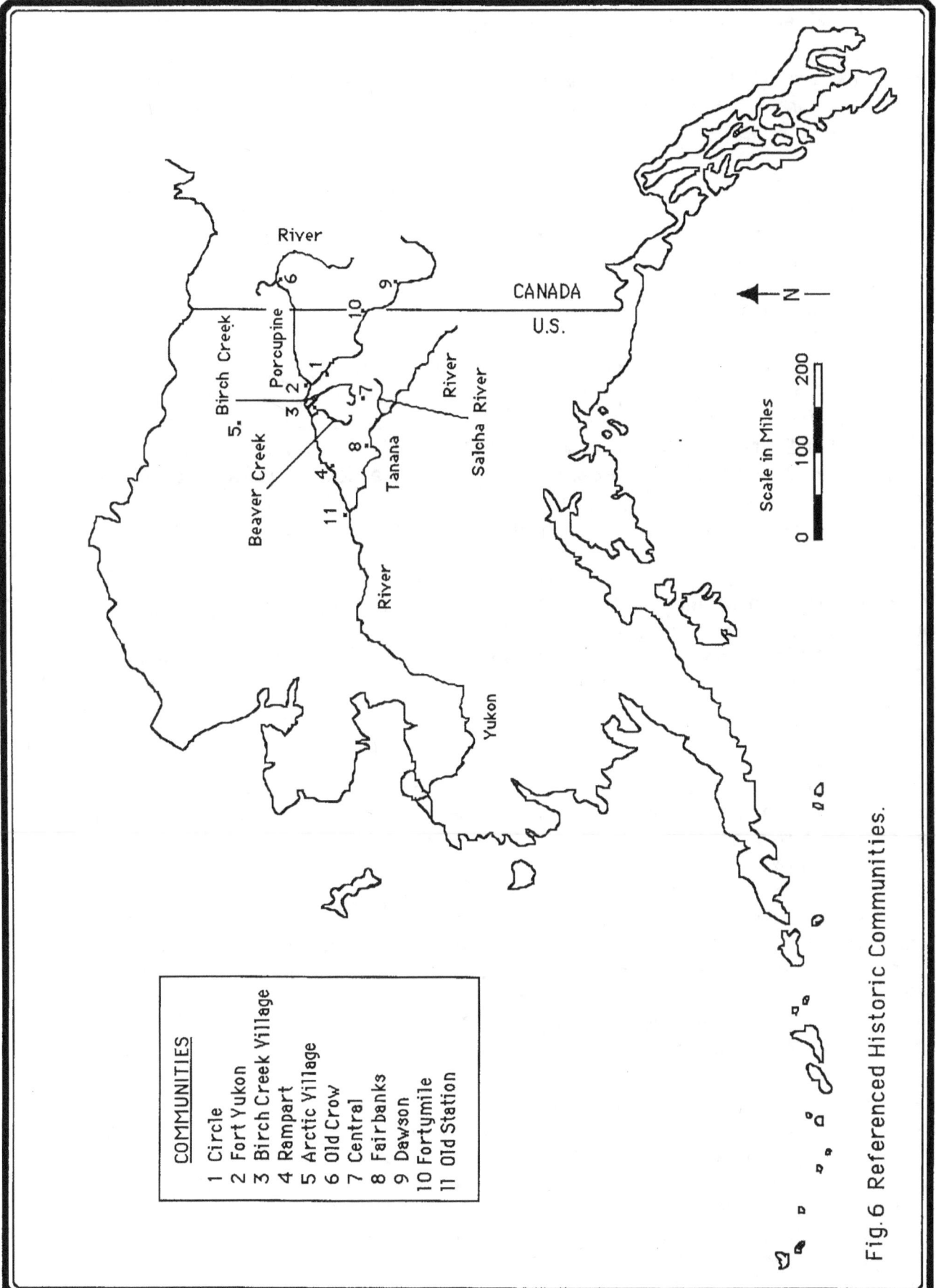

Fig. 6 Referenced Historic Communities.

COMMUNITIES

1 Circle
2 Fort Yukon
3 Birch Creek Village
4 Rampart
5 Arctic Village
6 Old Crow
7 Central
8 Fairbanks
9 Dawson
10 Fortymile
11 Old Station

15

The Kutchin or their immediate ancestors undoubtedly hunted caribou, either with the aid of dogs or with fences and snares, in the upland country drained by Beaver Creek. Caribou and sheep hunting may have been important enough to support a few camps along Beaver Creek. These small encampments would have been used as a base during the seasonal subsistence cycle.

During the summer, these camps may have been the location at which most fishing activity took place. Although salmon are not common to Beaver Creek, whitefish, grayling, northern pike, burbot, and sheefish were probably taken with traps (Osgood 1970:69 and 73). The Beaver Creek National Wild River flows into the Yukon where salmon could be taken in quantities. However, before the fish wheel was introduced by the white men, most fish were taken with traps in the smaller streams.

After drying and caching fish, the late summer and fall would be the time to prepare for caribou hunts in the neighboring uplands. Moose could be taken at any time. It seems likely that people would have made use of winter base camps during the coldest months and depend on their cached fish or caribou. In the lean times of late winter and early spring, beaver and muskrat became increasingly important as food sources, which would necessitate hunting in the smaller lakes and ponds in the Yukon Flats. The return of waterfowl to the Flats and their subsequent moult made them important prey in the early summer.

Of course, all wildlife resources are subject to cyclic fluctuations and changing migration patterns which at any time would result in feast or famine and varying human populations. One would expect to find fish camps of a few family or band members along the lower courses of major streams or the Yukon with satellite campsites or single hunting sites at strategic locations along Beaver Creek and in the adjacent uplands.

The earliest indication of travel in the Beaver Creek area comes from Schneider : "Another informant told me about his father who used to travel from Tanana up the Tanana River to the head of the Tolovana River, over the divide following the creek to Beaver Creek and then over to Fort Yukon" (Ibid. 1976:199).

Use of Beaver Creek itself above Victoria Creek was probably limited to fishing. During the summer months, it is not easily navigable above the mouth of Victoria Creek, due to variable water levels, and the upwelling of warm springs during the winter months which makes travel on the ice unsafe. However, trail heads into the uplands at such locations as the mouths of Victoria, Sheep, Willow, and Fossil Creeks may have been used from larger fishing camps lower down on Beaver Creek or on the Yukon.

These patterns would have been disrupted with the increased dependence on trade goods and fur trapping. A prime factor in the seasonal cycle would be trading, which, after its founding, usually meant being at Fort Yukon in the early summer. Increased dependence on furbearers meant set traplines and a greater need for fish, preferably salmon, to feed dogteams. The dogteams provided increased mobility and more extensive traplines with the fish camp becoming a more settled camp. The importance of caribou hunting probably declined with a greater emphasis being placed on moose as a food resource.

16

HISTORY

Early Exploration and Mining

In 1863, Reverand Robert McDonald accompanied two natives from Fort Yukon to a site called "Kotlo" where they claimed the earth screamed like a human voice. They traveled forty miles up the Yukon, crossed a portage to "Birch River" and descended the stream to a tributuary called "Kootlonjok". The stream was "craggy and shoaled" and it took a day to ascend to "Kotlo", a 100' high hill with a waterfall, crumbling earth and an abundance of fossils. McDonald found flakes of gold in a nearby stream (Ducker 1982:4).

Whymper(1868:227) reported that small amounts of gold had been found by some of the Hudson's Bay men near Fort Yukon but not enough to warrant a gold rush.

In 1873, Jack McQuesten and some companions built a winter camp at the mouth of Beaver Creek and prospected the vicinity. Although some gold was found, the quantities did not justify mining the area (Brooks 1953:316).

Minutes from a meeting of the "Beaver River Mining District" in May of 1900 strongly suggest that gold had been found in the upper part of Beaver Creek prior to the turn of the century; "the first recorder [went] to a foreign country and [took] the minutes and books of former meetings...." Nearly 60 claims were recorded in 1900 (Beaver River Mining District 1900).

According to Brooks, a first "gold rush" occurred in the Beaver Creek drainage during 1904:

> In the late summer a discovery of placer gold was reported to have been made near the mouth of what was named Golden [Victoria] Creek. This stream enters Beaver Creek from the west, near the edge of the Yukon Flats. As the main stream is navigable for small steamers to the junction with [Victoria Creek], the locality is easily accessible.
>
> About 211 men reached the locality before the winter set in, but no extensive prospecting was done. Good authorities state that the surface gravels yield half a cent to the pan. From another source it was learned that a 25-cent nugget had been found. No attempt was made last season to excavate to bed rock, which is probably very deep. Winter digging now going on will doubtless show whether this locality carries any workable placers. [Brooks 1905:29]

These prospectors came overland from Fairbanks and by boat from Circle (Stone 1906:131). Supplies were hauled in from Fort Hamlin via the head of Hess Creek during the winter of 1904-1905. Stone goes on to say that:

> Willow Creek, a stream about 15 miles long, which joins Beaver from the

south 10 miles above the point where it passes from the mountains into the flats, was staked along its upper course in August, 1904. Inscriptions on a tree indicated that there had been a small stampede, probably from the Fairbanks country, which had proved unprofitable. Some one seemed to have spent the winter on the creek and left in the spring of 1905. Bench gravels were seen 10 to 50 feet above the creek. [Ducker 1982: Ch.6, p. 69]

There is little record of active mining along Beaver Creek until 1910; when claims were developed on Trail, Ophir, and Nome Creeks (Ellsworth and Parker 1911:165).

During May, 1910, some good values were found on Ophir Creek, a tributary to Nome Creek, which resulted in starting a small stampede about the middle of July. All of the ground in the Nome and Trail Creek drainage basins was staked, as well as that on several other creeks near by. Systematic prospecting followed in the wake of the stampede, and if reports are to be relied upon, pay streaks have been located on Nome Creek above Ophir and on Ophir Creek near its mouth. Bedrock drains were being established on upper Nome Creek during the summer by an outfit which proposes to operate a bottomless team scraper next season. The ground is all shallow, averaging about 15 feet deep, with 2 to 4 feet of pay gravel, so that open-cut methods will no doubt prove to be the cheapest means of recovering the gold. Ophir Creek, which flows into Nome Creek about 2 miles from its mouth, was the scene of the liveliest excitement during the stampede. On Discovery claim a 50-foot cross cut was run to determine the width of the pay streak, and it is stated that this was traced for a length of five claims before the close of the open season. The gravel carries coarse gold valued at about $17 an ounce and is reported to run from $1.25 to $1.75 to the square foot. The largest nugget found was valued at $4.30. Some very encouraging deposits were found on Trail Creek, which heads opposite Poker Creek, flows for about 15 miles in a northeasterly direction, and joins Beaver Creek about 6 miles below Nome Creek. Prospects were also found on several newly named creeks, such as Dominion Creek, Gold Mountain Creek, and Hoosier Creek, the location of which was not learned by the writers.

Much complaint was made about the laws that made it possible for one man, with a power of attorney..., to stake association claims. It is said that 12 miles of creek were staked by one man in this manner. [Ellsworth and Parker 1911:150-151]

Other minerals found at Nome Creek include cassiterite, monazite, topaz, and tourmaline (Cobb 1973:174). In 1926 the Nome Creek Dredging Company built and began operating a dredge on Nome Creek which yielded $50,000 to $80,000 in gold annually until it was destroyed by fire in 1932. A dredge was moved into Nome Creek from Deadwood Creek in 1939 and worked there for two years. A few small plants using bulldozers, hydraulics, and draglines were at work during World War II on Beaver and Ophir Creeks. The dredge operated again on Nome Creek from 1945 to 1947 (Ducker 1982: Ch. 4, p. 24.)

Since 1975, upper Beaver Creek has been the site of increasing mining activity.

Travel and Transportation

Although Beaver Creek is generally navigable upstream as far as Victoria Creek, the first prospectors in 1904 came overland from Fairbanks as well as up Beaver Creek from the Yukon and Circle. Later that fall and winter, other
individuals brought in supplies from Fort Hamlin by coming over the headwaters of Hess Creek and across the divide to the headwaters of Victoria Creek, with one load weighing 3500 pounds (Ducker 1982: Ch. 7, P. 43).

The gold rush to the Chandalar country inspired the Alaska Road Commission (ARC) to allot $2500 for the location and construction of a winter sled trail overland from Chatanika to the community of Beaver on the Yukon. The crews spent the winters of 1909-1910 and 1910-1911 working on the route:

> These parties can work efficiently only after the ground freezes and before the heavy snow comes; this limits their working season very closely, and has made it necessary to extend the work over a long period. In addition to the actual location, the parties are charged with the construction of a narrow dog-sled trail. By January of 1912 the party completed all but 20 miles of the trail in the Victoria Creek area. The average cost of the road was $15 per mile and it was completed by the end of 1912. [Board of Road Commissioners of Alaska 1912:20]

With the demise of activity in the Chandalar district, the push for work on the trail subsided and, although $500 was allotted to repair bridges along the route in 1920, it did not prove feasible. In 1923 it was decided to relocate the southern portion of the route and it now started from Snowshoe, on the Olnes-Livengood sled road. From there it reached the Beaver trail about 26 miles from Snowshoe, followed the sides of Beaver Creek, crossed over the divide to the headwaters of Victoria Creek, and continued overland northward to Beaver. In 1924, this trail was brushed out by the ARC to a width of eight feet, bridges were built, and three stoves were installed in old cabins along the route (Ducker 1982: Ch. 7, p. 44). A 1931 map shows the route and six shelter cabins (Fig. 7). Most of this route is parallel to, rather than along Beaver Creek itself, undoubtedly due to the problem of warm springs and overflow on the Creek.

Other routes into Beaver Creek included the old ARC road from Chatanika to the Nome Dredging Company's operations on Nome Creek (Ibid:41), as well as a route from Mile 42 on the Steese Highway to Nome Creek four miles upstream from Beaver Creek. This is the route most often used today to get into Beaver Creek, although summer and winter trails maintained by BLM extend from Mile 28 and Mile 56 of the Elliott highway, respectively.

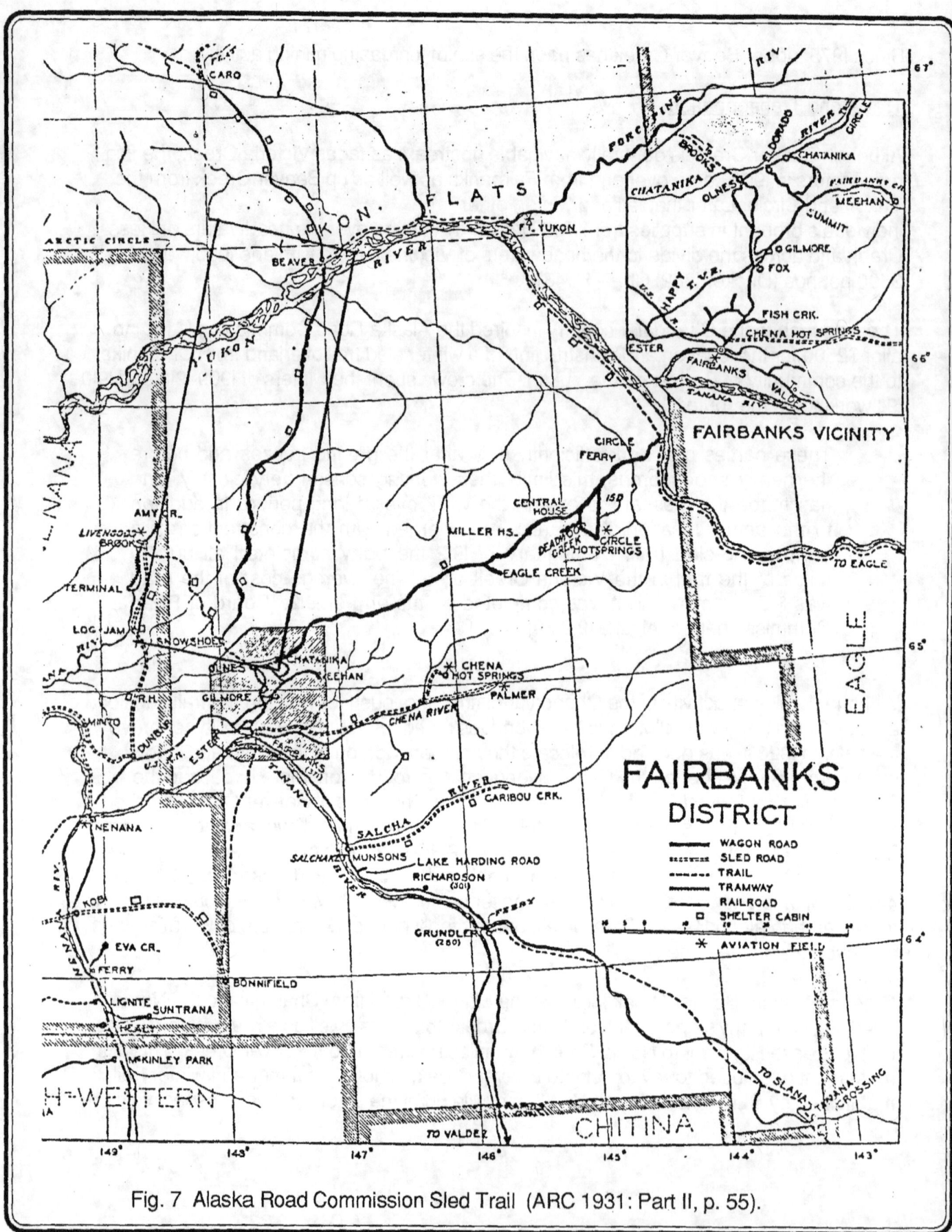

Fig. 7 Alaska Road Commission Sled Trail (ARC 1931: Part II, p. 55).

Summary

The little history that is known for Beaver Creek is dominated by mining activity. The small earlier gold rushes to Victoria, Trail, Ophir, and Nome Creek probably resulted in most individuals living in the country for the summer season only. They would have inhabited canvas tents, cooked on woodfires, and have spent most of their time working the creeks with gold pans, picks, shovels, and sluice boxes.

The few hardy individuals who wintered along Beaver Creek or its tributary valleys were likely to have spent the summers prospecting the country or operating their small scale mining operations and devoting the winters to trapping out of small log cabins which constituted home.

Later dredging and other large scale operations would have been seasonal with the workers employed only during the long summer days between breakup and freeze-up. Most of these individuals would have left the country at the end of the summer.

The building of the Chatanika-Beaver Trail which provided winter access between Fairbanks and the Yukon resulted in the establishment of six small roadhouses. These were simple shelter cabins where travelers and their dog teams could rest for the night.

CLASS II INVENTORY

Methodology

A Class II Inventory is defined as "a sample-oriented field inventory designed to locate and record, from surface and exposed profile indications, all cultural resource sites within a portion of a defined area in a manner which will allow an objective estimate of the nature and distribution of cultural resources in the entire defined area" (BLM 1978:3).

The primary purpose of the Beaver Creek survey was to locate evidence of historic and prehistoric use in the Beaver Creek National Wild River corridor.
Prior to the field survey, previous experience and knowledge was used to mark USGS topographic (1:63,360) maps with possible site areas on the basis of topography from existing aerial photographs, helicopter surveys undertaken during 1981 for the White Mountains National Recreation Area planning process, and data from the 1981 BLM historic cabin field inventory.

In addition, sites were sought in the field on the basis of past work in similar physiographic locales where sites have been found. In view of the size of the area and logistical problems involved, it was neither economical nor feasible to examine the entire range of landforms. Therefore, previous archeological knowledge and experience become the foundation of this judgmental type of sampling strategy, particulary since no prehistoric sites have been reported in the area. Kunz summarizes this type of survey:

> Much more time was spent surveying in potentially good areas than in potentially poor areas. The result is that sites which occur in the

potentially poor areas are less likely to be found. However, to reach areas of high archeological potential, the archeologist often has to cross areas of low archeological potential. While traversing low interest areas, the archeologist is still observing the ground, albeit in a hurried and cursory manner. In this way, areas of low archeological potential receive some coverage even if it is unplanned and uncoordinated. As a result, some of the less common types of sites were located and documented.

Given this sampling bias the information obtained from the survey should be useful from a general management and planning point of view. A general pattern of site density and distribution in the more easily traversed and hospitable portions of the study area was generated. These areas are of primary concern in terms of management and planning for the preserve as they are the locations most likely to be impacted by recreational use of road construction. Additionally, the surveyed areas should generate enough data to make some reasonable assumptions concerning land use, temporal range, and cultural affitiation of the prehistoric inhabitants of the region. [Kunz l984:4]

A Class II Inventory of the Beaver Creek National Wild River corridor was conducted June 25 through July 5, 1984. This was undertaken by Susan Will, the BLM Yukon Resource Area Archeologist, with assistance provided by Jo Feyhl, a recreation planner; and David Vogler, the Yukon Resource Area Hydrologist; both of whom had previously assisted in the Birch Creek Class II cultural resources inventory. The river was floated from the confluence of Beaver and Nome Creeks to a point three miles below the confluence of Beaver and Victoria Creeks. Potential locations for examination were hiked to from the river and tested.

Since the Beaver Creek National Wild River corridor is less than 5 miles wide, with the exception of some of the river floodplain, most of the corridor was visible from the river. Much of the route cuts through hills and the edges of the White and Victoria Mountains which allows viewing up the hillsides from the river itself.

Results

Approximately 75% of the Beaver Creek National Wild River corridor, with the exception of some of the low country which could not be seen from the river, was examined visually from the river. Thirty-four locations (Fig. 8) were examined on foot and/or trowel-tested on the basis of judgemental site potential, vegetation density, and physical accessibility. Most of these locations were located adjacent to or overlooking the river and averaged about l/2-acre in size. In the cases where there were edges of "bluffs" or "cutbanks" the upper edges were walked and tested and the bases were also examined. Gravel bars were walked over and visually examined.

Two historic cabin locations, previously reported by the l98l BLM survey, were also examined, primarily to make location checks.

One site was discovered.

It is on a small terrace of moss and heather with scraggly spruce trees on the hillside just above it to the north. The promontory just south of it across the drainage creek is what initially attracted attention as a potential hunting lookout and the association of the hearth to this promontory indicates that it may have been a temporary camp for moose hunters. The site's proximity to the landing strip across the river also suggests a recent white hunter's camp, although most white hunters camp on gravel bars or in the spruce stands along the river's edge. The site consists of a moss-grown hearth. There is partially burnt wood poking out of the moss and small pieces of charcoal beneath it. The southeast quarter of the pit was excavated to a depth of about 3"; down to bedrock. A layer of ash, less than l" thick was visible beneath the moss. Within a foot of the hearth and north of it is a pile of weathered wood and the area extending approximately 2' around the hearth is level although overgrown with moss. Neither cultural material nor bone was found either at the site nor on the adjacent promontory. Due to the distinct appearance of the moss in the hearth, and the presence of the adjacent wood, the site appears to be rather recent.

MANAGEMENT RECOMMENDATIONS

In view of the fact that there is very little ethnohistorical information pertaining directly to the Beaver Creek National Wild River corridor and that no prehistoric material was discovered during l0 days of field survey, the potential for discovery of prehistoric sites within the river corridor does not appear great. However, the literature search indicates that the surrounding country had been used by man in the past and it is likely that the river corridor may also have been used. As a result, any site which may be discovered would be important.

One possible reason for the lack of sites adjacent to the river may be a result of the active geologic faults and subsequent erosion taking place along the river's present course. In addition, with the exception of the river's upper reaches (above the Big Bend) and the section from Victoria Creek into the Flats, there are very few Quaternary-aged deposits overlying the bedrock along Beaver Creek within the corridor. Sites located along the river's edge may have eroded away. Most of the possible locations for sites which were examined turned out to be either on actively eroding bluffs or located further back from the river's edge where the dense vegetative cover would require extensive work for site discovery. The potential for site occurrence appears greater in the upper reaches of the corridor where Quaternary overburden exists.

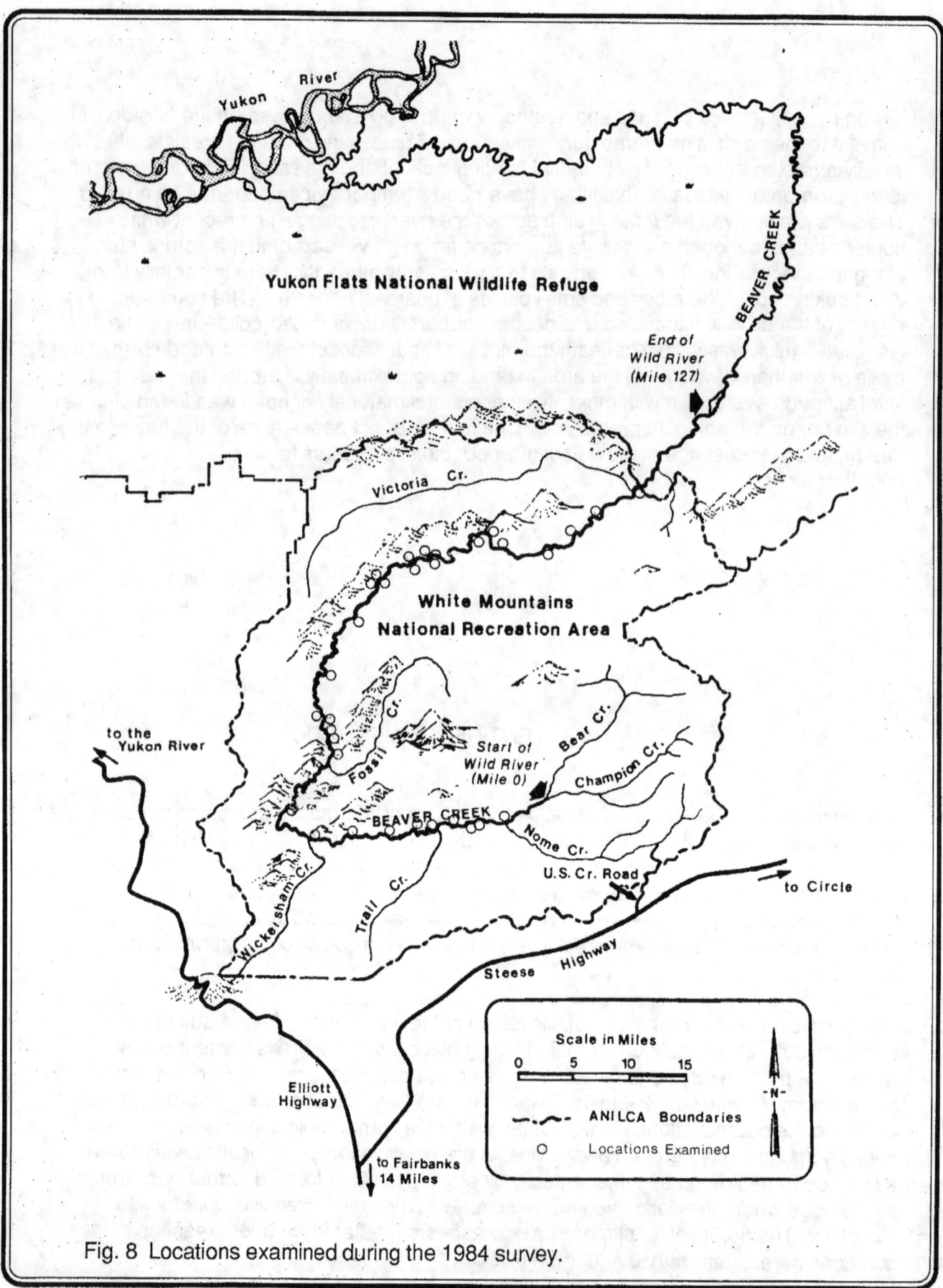

Fig. 8 Locations examined during the 1984 survey.

Since the management plan for the Beaver Creek National Wild River corridor does not encourage development which would have surface disturbing activity, it is unlikely that there would be a significant impact on prehistoric cultural or paleontological resources. However, due to the limited nature of the Class II field inventory, any development which might involve surface disturbance would require more extensive testing for subsurface cultural resources. Visitor impact will probably be highest along the river itself and most potential prehistoric site locations away from the river are protected by vegetation.

The discovery of the single site was inadvertent, found while walking to the promontory near it. This is important in the fact that it indicates that such areas should be carefully examined in the future if surface disturbing impacts do take place. The potential for other impacts to such sites are not significant, as the vegetation and lack of active erosion at such locations provides a natural protection.

It is possible that ongoing mining activity may impact cultural or paleontological resources which would not be readily identifiable during reconnaissance level surveys. Monitoring of mining and other activities within the corridor will help identify as yet undiscovered cultural and paleontological resources.

The seven historic cabin sites located in the corridor are susceptible to impacts from visitor use. People are attracted to old cabins. Although only three of these are visible from the river, several of the others are marked on the USGS maps. Most of them are in advanced stages of natural decay and there is very little in the way of important artifacts associated with them. These cabins are not "significant" in the strictly legal sense but they are locally important from a cultural and recreational standpoint. They form an integral part of man's association with Beaver Creek and provide visitors with an indication of the country's history.

Since much of the historic sites' importance has to do with visitor use, the best management of these resources would be to incorporate them into a visitor use plan. Future management of the Beaver Creek National Wild River corridor precludes the construction of new shelter cabins, yet the river is used by recreational floaters, fisherman, and fall and winter hunters, some of whom use the river as an access point to the surrounding country. Without making significant alterations, several of these existing cabins could be reconstructed or stabilized to make them usable for shelter. Additional information provided in literature, posted signs, and cleaning up the sites could enhance visitors' experiences, improve their appreciation of Beaver Creek's cultural resources, and promote their understanding of the part such resources played Alaska's past.

REFERENCES CITED

Ager, Thomas A.
    1975   *Late Quaternary Environmental History of the Tanana Valley, Alaska.* Institute of Polar Studies Report No. 54. The Ohio State University Research Foundation, Columbus, Ohio.

Baker, Marcus
    1901   *Geographic Dictionary of Alaska.* U.S. Geological Survey Bulletin No. 187. U.S. Government Printing Office, Washington, D.C.

Barker, James C.
    1978   *Mineral Deposits of the Tanana-Yukon Uplands: A Summary Report.* Open File Report No. 88-78, U.S. Bureau of Mines, Fairbanks, Alaska.

Beaver River Mining District
    1900   Fairbanks Recorder's Office, Fairbanks, Alaska.

Board of Road Commissioners of Alaska
    1912   *Annual Report Upon the Construction of Military and Post Roads, Bridges, and Trails; and of Other Roads, Tramways, Ferries, Bridges, Trails and Related Works In the Territory of Alaska.* Daily Empire Printing, Juneau, Alaska.

    1913   *Annual Report Upon the Construction of Military and Post Roads, Bridges, and Trails; and of Other Roads, Tramways, Ferries, Bridges, Trails, and Related Works In the Territory of Alaska.* Daily Empire Printing, Juneau, Alaska.

    1931   *Annual Report Upon the Construction of Military and Post Roads, Bridges, and Trails; and of Other Roads, Tramways, Ferries, Bridges, Trails and Related Works in the Territory of Alaska, Part II.* Daily Empire Printing, Juneau, Alaska.

Brooks, Alfred H.
1905   Placer Mining in Alaska in 1904. In *Report on Progress of
            Investigations of Mineral Resources of Alaska in
            1904,* edited by Alfred H. Brooks and others, pp. 18-31.
            U.S. Geological Survey Bulletin No. 259. U.S. Government Printing
            Office, Washington, D.C.

1973   *Blazing Alaska's Trails.* Reprinted. University of Alaska
            Press, Fairbanks. Originally published 1953, University of
            Alaska Press, Fairbanks, Alaska.

Bureau of Land Management
1978   *BLM Manual 8100 - Cultural Resource Management.*
            U.S. Department of the Interior, Washington, D.C.

1983   *River Management Plan for the Beaver Creek National
            Wild River.* Bureau of Land Management and the Fish and
            Wildlife Service, U.S. Department of the Interior, Fairbanks,
            Alaska.

Caulfield, Richard A.
1983   *Subsistence Land Use in Upper Yukon-Porcupine
            Communities, Alaska.* Technical Paper Number 16, Alaska
            Department of Fish and Game Subsistence Division, Fairbanks,
            Alaska.

Caulfield, Richard A., Walter J. Peter, Clarence Alexander, and Katherine Peter
1983   *Gwich'in Athabaskan Place Names of the Upper
            Yukon-Porcupine Region, Alaska: A Preliminary Report.*
            Technical Paper Number 83, Alaska Department of Fish and Game
            Subsistence Division, Fairbanks, Alaska.

Chapmen, Robert M., Florence R. Weber, and Bond Taber
1971   *Preliminary Geologic Map of the Livengood Quadrangle,
            Alaska.* U.S. Geological Survey Open File Map No. 483, U.S.
            Government Printing Office, Washington, D.C.

Cobb, E.H.
1973   *Placer Deposits of Alaska.* U.S. Geological Survey Bulletin No.
            1374. U.S. Government Printing Office, Washington, D.C.

Cook, John P.
  1975   Archeology of Interior Alaska. *The Western Canadian Journal
                of Anthropology* (5) 3-4:125-133.

Davis, J.L., R. Shideler and R.E. LeResche
  1978   *Fortymile Caribou Herd Studies.* Pittman Robertson Projects
                W-17-6 and W-17-7, Final Report. Alaska Department of
                Fish and Game, Fairbanks, Alaska.

Ducker, James H.
  1982   *Alaska's Upper Yukon: A History.* Unpublished Ms., Bureau of
                Land Management, Anchorage, Alaska.

Durtsche, B.M.
  1983   *Interim Report - Distribution of Caribou in the White
                Mountains, 1982-83.* Open File Report. Bureau of Land
                Management, Fairbanks, Alaska.

Ellsworth, C.E., and G.L. Parker
  1911   Placer Mining in the Yukon-Tanana Region. In *Mineral
                Resources of Alaska: Report on Progress of
    Investigation in 1910* , edited by Alfred H. Brooks and others,
                pp. 153-172. U.S. Geological Survey Bulletin No. 480. U.S.
                Government Printing Office, Washington, D.C.

Guthrie, R.D.
  1968   Paleoecology of a Late Pleistocene Small Mammal Community
                From Interior Alaska. *Arctic Journal of the Arctic Institute
                of North America* 21(4):223-244.

Hopkins, David M. (editor)
  1967   *The Bering Land Bridge.* Stanford University Press, Palo Alto,
                California.

Kunz, Michael L., Peter G. Phippen, Richard E. Reanier and Mark Standley
  1984   *Upper Kobuk River Drainage: Draft Report of Phase I of A
                Cultural Resources Survey and Inventory in Gates of the
                Arctic National Park and Preserve.* Gates of the Arctic
                National Park and Preserve, National Park Service, Fairbanks,
                Alaska.

Le Blanc, Raymond Joseph
    1984   *The Rat Indian Creek Site and the Late Prehistoric Period in the Interior Northern Yukon.* Archaeological Survey of Canada Paper No. 120, National Museum of Man Mercury Series. National Museums of Canada, Ottawa.

McKennan, Robert A.
    1969   Athapaskan Groups of Central Alaska at the Time of White Contact. *Ethnohistory* 16(4):335-343.

Morlan, Richard E.
    1973   *The Later Prehistory of the Middle Porcupine Drainage, Northern Yukon Territory.* Archaeological Survey of Canada Paper No. 11, National Museum of Man Mercury Series. National Museums of Canada, Ottawa.

Murie, Olaus J.
    1953   *Alaska-Yukon Caribou.* North American Fauna No. 4. U.S. Department of Agriculture, Washington, D.C.

Nelson, Richard K.
    1973   *Hunters of the Northern Forest.* University of Chicago Press, Chicago.

Osgood, Cornelius
    1970   *Contributions to the Ethnology of the Kutchin.* Yale University Publications in Anthropology No. 14. Human Relations File, New Haven.

Prindle, L.M.
    1913   *A Geologic Reconnaissance of the Fairbanks Quadrangle, Alaska.* U.S. Geological Survey Bulletin No. 525. U.S. Government Printing Office, Washington, D.C.

Schneider, William
    1974   *Interview with Birch Creek Jimmy on 2/27, 2/28, and 3/01/74.* Ms. in possession of author.

    1976   *Beaver, Alaska: The Story of a Multi-Ethnic Community.* Unpublished Ph.D. dissertation, Department of Anthropology, Bryn Mawr College, Bryn Mawr, Pennsylvannia.

Skoog, Ronald O.

1956   *Range, Movements, Population, and Food habits of the Steese--Fortymile Caribou Herd.* Unpublished Master's thesis, University of Alaska, Fairbanks.

Stone, R.W.

1906   Reconnaissance from Circle to Fort Hamlin. In *Report on Progress of Investigations of Mineral Resources of Alaska in 1905*, edited by Alfred H. Brooks and others, pp. . U.S. Geological Survey Bulletin No. 284. Government Printing Office, Washington, D.C.

Thorson, Robert M., and Thomas D. Hamilton

1977   Geology of the Dry Creek Site: A Stratified Early Man Site in Interior Alaska. *Quaternary Research* 7:149-176.

West, Frederick Hadleigh

1981   *The Archeology of Beringia.* Columbia University Press, New York.

Whymper, Frederick

1966   *Travel and Adventure in the Territory of Alaska.* Reprinted. Readex Microprint. Originally published 1868, John Murray, London.

Will, Susan M.

1984   *Beaver Creek National Wild River Class I Inventory.* Bureau of Land Management, Fairbanks, Alaska.

Appendix

BEAVER CREEK CABIN INVENTORY

CABIN SITE NUMBER: 1

MAP REFERENCE:

RECORDED BY: Stephen Young

LOCATION:

DATE: 7/29/82

SETTING: Located next to Beaver Creek on the south bank just after an old island (now a large gravel bar) on the left (south).

TOPOGRAPHY: Level, sits about 6 feet above the creek.

VEGETATION: Clear around the cabin and cache with small white birch, grasses and berries, surrounded by a spruce and white birch forest.

BUILDINGS: 2

SIZES: cabin - 9' by 9'
        cache - 4' by 4' (top part)

TYPES: Cabin and cache.

WINDOWS: 1; 1.5' by 1.5'

DOORS: 1; 2.5' wide (height could not be determined because of ruined condition)

ROOMS: 1

FOUNDATION: earth

ROOFING: collapsed; was probably sod

OTHER: logs unpeeled and saw-cut

CONDITION: Poor; roof fallen in, one wall standing two partially.

ARTIFACTS, EQUIPMENT, OBJECTS IN OR AROUND STRUCTURES: Yukon stove (destroyed), old lantern, woodpile, coffee and powdered milk cans, spice can, bed shelves, broken glass from window.

ADDITIONAL INFORMATION ABOUT CABIN SITE: Cache can be seen from the creek but the cabin cannot.

7/29/82 Full shot of the east side of Beaver Creek Cabin Site #1.

7/29/82 Inside of Cabin #1 showing shelves and window.

BEAVER CREEK CABIN INVENTORY

CABIN SITE NUMBER: 2   MAP REFERENCE:

RECORDED BY: Stephen Young   LOCATION:

DATE: 7/29/82

SETTING: Located on the north bank of a meander of Beaver Creek. It cannot be seen from the river.

TOPOGRAPHY: Level, up about 8 feet from the meander.

VEGETATION: Cabin area is surrounded by a spruce forest, the immediate area around the cabin had grasses, berries, and small hardwoods.

BUILDINGS: 1   SIZES: 9' by 10'

TYPES: Cabin, unpeeled spruce logs.   WINDOWS: 1; 2' by .5'

DOORS: 1   ROOMS: 1

FOUNDATION: earth   ROOFING: collapsed; was probably sod

OTHER: No other structures visible in the area.   CONDITION: Very poor.

ARTIFACTS, EQUIPMENT, OBJECTS IN OR AROUND STRUCTURES: Nothing non-organic in the area.

ADDITIONAL INFORMATION ABOUT CABIN SITE:

7/29/82 View of Cabin Site #2 from the side - looking to the northwest from the back.

7/29/82 Cabin #2 from the rear - looking west toward Beaver Creek.

BEAVER CREEK CABIN INVENTORY

CABIN SITE NUMBER: 3   MAP REFERENCE:

RECORDED BY: Stephen Young   LOCATION:

DATE: 7/30/82

SETTING: Located on the north bank of Beaver Creek above a large gravel bar.

TOPOGRAPHY: Sits on level land, about 7' above the present water level.

VEGETATION: Open area around the cabin, surrounded by a tall (for this area) spruce forest.

BUILDINGS: 1   SIZES: 18' by 18'

TYPES: Log cabin of unpeeled spruce logs.   WINDOWS: none

DOORS: 1   ROOMS: 1

FOUNDATION: earth   ROOFING: Flat boards - crudely cut; probably done
                                         by the person from the cabin.

OTHER: CONDITION: Fair, 3 sides standing; one starting to
                                         crumble; roof caved in but boards are still visible.

ARTIFACTS, EQUIPMENT, OBJECTS IN OR AROUND STRUCTURES: One stove and piping, one wooden
barrel (very rotten): labeled "(something) Steel Co. 100 lbs." Possible contained nails.

ADDITIONAL INFORMATION ABOUT CABIN SITE: Cabin site just visible from the water.

7/30/82 View of the north side of Cabin #3 (what may have been the doorway?). Beaver Creek in the background.

7/30/82 Stove outside of Cabin #3.

BEAVER CREEK CABIN INVENTORY

CABIN SITE NUMBER: 4

MAP REFERENCE:

RECORDED BY: Stephen Young

LOCATION:

DATE: 7/30/82

SETTING: Located on the south side of Beaver Creek, across from Big Bend, a couple of hundred yards back in the woods.

TOPOGRAPHY: Flat, lowlands.

VEGETATION: Primarily spruce with some hardwoods, birch, aspen, and some grasses.

BUILDINGS: 1

SIZES: ?

TYPES: Cache with 12' ladder

WINDOWS:

DOORS:

ROOMS:

FOUNDATION: on stilts

ROOFING: wood

OTHER:

CONDITION: In total disrepair, in pieces on the ground.

ARTIFACTS, EQUIPMENT, OBJECTS IN OR AROUND STRUCTURES: One stove (square), coffee pot, jar with what looked like rice in it, porcelain pot, Hills Bros. coffee can (red can brand), 12' ladder.

ADDITIONAL INFORMATION ABOUT CABIN SITE: This site was very difficult to find. We thought what we found was a cache because we found the stilts with metal bands, a ladder, and the logs were too small for a cabin. Searched the area for a cabin but did not find one.

7/30/82 Shot of cache remains at Cabin Site #4.

7/30/82 The cache ladder at Cabin Site #4.

BEAVER CREEK CABIN INVENTORY

CABIN SITE NUMBER: 5

MAP REFERENCE:

RECORDED BY: Stephen Young

LOCATION:

DATE: 7/31/82

SETTING: On the west (eroding) bank of Beaver Creek.

TOPOGRAPHY: Level land just above the river.

VEGETATION: Cabin is in an open field, surrounded by a spruce forest.

BUILDINGS: 1

SIZES: 14.5' by 14.5'

TYPES: Unpeeled spruce log cabin.

WINDOWS: 2; 2.5' high by 2' wide

DOORS: 1; 4.5' high by 2.5' wide

ROOMS: 1

FOUNDATION: earth

ROOFING: sod; 4" diameter poles, birch bark, tin, and topped with sod.

OTHER: Floor of mill-cut wood planks.

CONDITION: Fair to good.

ARTIFACTS, EQUIPMENT, OBJECTS IN OR AROUND STRUCTURES: Inside was full of all kinds of stuff: 1967 magazome. books (heavy reading - Civil Disobedience, poetry, etc. - tent, water color paintings on the walls, stove, pots and pans, plastic flowers, drapes and other such stuff. We also found a stack of postcards with the name of a person printed on each one: Mrs. Frederick W. Campbell.

ADDITIONAL INFORMATION ABOUT CABIN SITE: Visible from the river. All of us felt that the person who lived here was most likely a woman. There might have been a man living with her, but we were not sure. She was probably out to experience the wilderness more so than trapping and mining. We felt this because of the feminine touches to the place, and the books left behind. Neat (interesting) cabin!

7/31/82 Looking at the front Cabin #5 from the river bank.

7/31/82 Door of Cabin #5 - note the pelt used for insulation.

BEAVER CREEK CABIN INVENTORY

CABIN SITE NUMBER: 6

MAP REFERENCE:

RECORDED BY: Stephen Young

LOCATION:

DATE: 7/31/82

SETTING: On top of an eroding stream bank; northeast of Beaver Creek.

TOPOGRAPHY: Flat, open field.

VEGETATION: Open field, grasses, berries, small hardwoods, surrounded by spruces.

BUILDINGS: 1

SIZES: 12' by 17'

TYPES: Cabin; unpeeled spruce logs adzed flat
on the inside

WINDOWS: 1

DOORS: 1; 2.5' wide by 5' high

ROOMS: 1

FOUNDATION: Earth

ROOFING: Sod, caving in.

OTHER:

CONDITION: Fair to good, the roof is caving in (a
tree fell on the roof).

ARTIFACTS, EQUIPMENT, OBJECTS IN OR AROUND STRUCTURES: Stove, Hills Bros. coffee cans, a raft
and paddles, pots, pans, iron skillet, hip waders, and a 12' ladder.

ADDITIONAL INFORMATION ABOUT CABIN SITE:

44

7/31/82 Side/front of Cabin #6 showing roof decay and log fallen across it.

7/31/82 Side view of Beaver Creek Cabin #6.

BEAVER CREEK CABIN INVENTORY

CABIN SITE NUMBER: 7   MAP REFERENCE:

RECORDED BY: Stephen Young   LOCATION:

DATE: 8/02/82

SETTING: In a spruce forest about 20 yards from Beaver Creek.

TOPOGRAPHY: Mostly flat.

VEGETATION: Spruce forest.

BUILDINGS: 1   SIZES: ?

TYPES: Cache   WINDOWS:

DOORS: ROOMS:

FOUNDATION: four stilts with metal bands. ROOFING: Poles and canvas.

OTHER: CONDITION: Very poor, in pieces on the ground.

ARTIFACTS, EQUIPMENT, OBJECTS IN OR AROUND STRUCTURES: A rubber boat, some canvas, unpeeled spruce poles.

ADDITIONAL INFORMATION ABOUT CABIN SITE: Not on the topo map. Poor shape but the ladder still remains along the river bank so you can climb up to it. Not much to it at all.

8/02/82   View of the cache remains at Cabin Site #7 (looking to the south).

8/02/82   Ladder along the river bank which leads up to the cache.